Best wishes of
good weather
from the
author

Ian Currie

25/2/98.

Red Sky At Night

Weather Sayings For All Seasons

by Ian Currie, Edited by Mark Davison

Illustrations by Sue Attwood

Red Sky At Night

Weather Sayings For All Seasons

by Ian Currie, Edited by Mark Davison

Illustrations by Sue Attwood

First Edition 1992
Revised June 1995
© Copyright 1992 Frosted Earth

Published by Frosted Earth,
77 Rickman Hill,
Coulsdon, Surrey, CR5 3DT

Tel 01737 554869 or 01737 221215

Typeset by Vitaset, Paddock Wood, Kent
Printed by Litho Techniques, Godstone Road, Whyteleafe, Surrey

ISBN 0-9516710-2-2

About the Author

The ever-changing moods and patterns of our skies have always fascinated Ian Currie.

Childhood memories of the great thunderstorm of September 1958 and the big freeze of 1962-3 are still vivid in his mind . . . as are the blizzards of 1987 and the hurricane force winds of the same year.

Formerly a teacher and now a full time writer, forecaster and speaker, Ian's predictions are heard daily in Surrey, Sussex and Hampshire on County Sound and Radio Mercury. His popular weekly weather column has appeared for several years in the Surrey Mirror, Surrey Comet and the Sutton Herald Series.

At his talks to clubs and societies, many people ask what truth there is, if any, in weather sayings. Is a red sky at night a shepherd's delight? Will it rain if cows are lying down? What if the heavens open on St Swithin's Day. Will it be wet for 40 days?

Ian, a graduate in Earth Science and Geography, lives at Coulsdon, Surrey and is a Fellow of the Royal Meteorological Society. In this fascinating book he looks at weather sayings . . . and concludes that some are very wise, while others are nothing but old wives' tales.

Other Books by Ian Currie

The Surrey Weather Book: ISBN 0-9516710-1-4 £7.50
Written by Mark Davison and Ian Currie and published by Frosted Earth.

Surrey in the Hurricane: ISBN 0-9513019-2-6 £7.50
Written by Mark Davison and Ian Currie
London's Hurricane: ISBN 0-9513019-3-4 £7.95
Written by Mark Davison and Ian Currie
Both published by Froglets.

The following jointly published by Frosted Earth/Froglets and co-written by Currie, Davison and Ogley:

The Kent Weather Book: ISBN 1-872337-35-X £9.95
The Sussex Weather Book: ISBN 1-872337-30-9 £9.95
The Essex Weather Book: ISBN 1-872337-66-X £9.95

Introduction

Whether the weather be cold
Or whether the weather be hot,
We'll weather the weather
Whatever the weather,
Whether we like it or not.

From our earliest childhood days we learn that red skies at night mean shepherd's delight or that open pine cones bode fine weather. We are told that rain on St Swithin's day brings a spell of wet weather that will last 40 days and that lightning cannot strike the same place twice.

Even the moon has been accused of altering our weather. But is all this true? Or can we simply say:

The moon and the weather may change together
But a change in the moon does not change the weather.
And if there were no moon at all,
And that may seem strange,
We'd still have weather that's subject to change.

There are three ways to produce a weather forecast. First, one can use all that is available to modern science including super computers that can calculate 16 thousand million operations per second and can successfully predict what is going to happen a week ahead.

Secondly one could rely entirely on weather lore and predict a harsh winter from the amount of hips and haws seen or 'if the sun sets clear on Wednesday, expect fine weather for the rest of the week'.

There is a third way. Combine the two. Take a little elementary meterology, go out and look at the sky, use only the tried and tested prognosticators and apply to the local area. And there you have it, a reliable inexpensive method.

It has been said that a proverb is a folk saying which embodies one man's wit and all men's wisdom. One needs a sense of humour to make the best of our capricious weather. Even the finest day can have the dampener put on it:

> *Never trust a clear blue sky,*
> *Even if the glass points high.*

On the other hand:

> *Rain before seven,*
> *Dry before eleven.*

Perhaps we should heed the French:

> *Attendez à la nuit pour dire que le jour a été beau*

That is, wait till night before saying it has been a fine day.

But in all my weather watching, there is one thing that never varies no matter how hard I tap the barometer:

The glass is falling hour by hour,
The glass will fall forever,
But if you break the bloomin' glass,
You won't hold up the weather.

This book is a monthly guide to weather lore. Some sayings apply all year round whilst others are specific to a month or season. Most of them can be divided into three main groups. Firstly, those based on observation by people whose jobs were closely in touch with the weather. People like farmers and sailors. Secondly, weather maxims based on flowers, plants and animals whose behaviour can often be very weather-sensitive. And thirdly, the characteristic weather of saints' days or other special times of the year.

It was Samuel Johnson who wrote:

When two Englishmen meet, their first talk is of the weather.

With our country 'lying at the crossroads of the world's weather' and 'not having a climate – only weather' it is not surprising that as a nation we are particularly conscious of the elements and have built up a rich store of saws and sayings. Some are contradictory, others dubious but a few are very useful and most are amusing.

Every wind has its weather.

3

January

The belching winter wind, the missile rain,
the rare and welcome silence of the snows.

Although we may curse and grumble when having to scrape the ice off the car on a cold and dark January morning, mild weather of any duration is frowned upon in just about all weather lore. For it encourages insect pests to survive, is often very wet and forces plant growth which is then likely to be severely checked by frost in late winter or spring.

There is nothing so forlorn as a magnolia after a sharp early April frost.

If the grass grows in Janiveer,
it grows the worse for 't all the year.

or

"Better to see a mad dog than a hot sun in January"

5

One hears also that:

A cold January is followed by a hot summer

But there is no real truth in this. We can look back on January 1963, the coldest since 1814 and snow lay throughout. The following summer was far from auspicious with August being particularly dull and cool.

Often January displays a volatile, transient temperament and it is the weather watcher possessing a barometer who is less likely to be caught out.

Look at the dial. Rising air pressure generally indicates improving weather. A falling needle indicates worsening conditions. If you give it a tap and nothing changes, the current conditions outside are likely to continue.

When the glass falls low,
Prepare for a blow.
When the glass rises high,
Let the light duck fly.

If the pressure falls slowly but steadily, prolonged poor weather may follow whereas a short but sudden fall, although a sign of squally winds and heavy rain, is soon over.

Long foretold, long past,
Short warning, won't last

January sometimes displays a distinctly stormy disposition, none more so than on 25th January 1990 when the famous Burns Day storm felled four million trees in Britain. The centre of the storm crossed his birth place in Ayrshire.

'Was five and twenty days begun,
'Twas thae a blast o' Janwar win;
Blew hansel in on Robin

Robert (Robin) Burns

6

Winds were at their strongest when the air pressure started to rise quickly from a very low point. This also happened in the great October 1987 storm when 15 million trees were brought down.

First rise after a low
foretells a stronger blow.

One man did try to predict weather for the whole year of 1838. His name was Patrick Murphy and in particular, he singled out 20th January 1838 as being especially cold and inclement. How right he was. The day was exceptionally severe. At Cobham, Surrey, the frost was so sharp there was no quicksilver to be seen in Lady Moore's thermometer and a sheep was roasted whole on the ice of the Medway at Maidstone. Mr Murphy became an instant success.

Murphy has a weather eye,
He can tell whene'er he pleases:
Whether it's wet or whether it's dry,
Whether it's hot or whether it freezes.

Unfortunately, he tried to do the same for the following year, but his predictions were a dismal failure and he fled into obscurity – just as many long range weather forecasters have done since!

Murphy promises frost, it turns out to be snow,
The wind's fast asleep when he tells us it will blow,
For his rain we get sunshine, for high we have low,
Yet he swears he's infallible weather or no!

 # February

One of my favourite sayings tells us:

> *If Candlemas be fair and bright,*
> *Winter will have another flight,*
> *If Candlemas be shower and rain,*
> *Winter is gone and will not come again.*

andlemas is now on 2nd February and Scandinavian weather lore tells us that 'as the day lengthens, the cold strengthens'. Certainly for southern England during the 1980s and early 1990s, February has become the coldest month. Both these sayings indicate that winter can be late. Indeed, some famous winters such as 1855, 1895 and 1947 really intensified during February.

More recently, 1986 was an icy month. At Buxton in Derbyshire, the mercury only rose above freezing for just a few minutes during the whole month.

February 1991 will be remembered for 'the wrong type of snow' — a description given to the powdery flakes by British Rail after it brought trains to a halt in southern England.

The reason for February's chill is that the sea and atmosphere cool down gradually during winter and reach their coldest levels in this month. The warming effect of our surrounding sea is at its least. Scandinavia, Russia and the Arctic experience their thickest ice in February, so there is much truth in the saying:

> *When the wind is in the east,*
> *'Tis neither good for man or beast.*

Another saying especially attributed to February runs:

> *February fill dyke*
> *Be it black or be it white*
> *But if it be white, it's better to like.*

9

"When the wind is in the East tis neither good for Man nor beast"

his does not mean that it is a wet month. In fact, it is so often one of the driest. But in February and the other winter months, evaporation is low and ground water is replenished. The water table rises to fill the ditches and ponds and increase the flow in our rivers.

A snow cover in February protects the land from the worst excesses of frost and snow, and a slow thaw gently releases the water into the ground. A sudden thaw accompanied by heavy rain is one of the most damaging of weather combinations. Such conditions occurred in 1900 when in mid February, Guildford town bridge in Surrey was badly damaged by the turbulent waters of the River Wey.

Any time in winter during settled spells, a cloudless sky at night is a sign that temperatures below freezing can be expected. Hence the adage:

"Clear moon, frost soon"

"March comes in like a lion and goes out like a lamb"

March

Daffodils
That came before the swallow dares, and take
The winds of March with beauty

Shakespeare

A peck of March dust is worth its weight in gold.

After the dampness of winter a dry spell is often welcomed by farmers and gardeners alike so that the land can be worked. This was none more so than in 1995 when the winter was exceptionally wet and after mid month an area of high pressure did build to give some welcome relief from the rains.

Probably one of the best known of all weather sayings applies to this month:

March comes in like a lion
But goes out like a lamb

The decade of the 1980s saw no such pattern and in 1991 the month began and ended in a calm. Weather lore bodes ill for the end of the month:

March borrows of April
Three days and they be ill;
April borrows of March again
Three days of wind and rain

Often poor weather rounds off March and continues into April. In 1994 winds gusted to 50 to 60 mph with heavy driving rain on the last evening whilst in 1952 after a quiet start the month ended in blinding snowstorms with drifts 15 feet deep in the Chilterns almost an illustration of 'If the birds sing before St. David's Day they will be silent by Lady Day'.

March weather can be extraordinarily variable as can April and it is said: 'March changes seven times a day', a description that characterised many days during this month in 1995. An unknown 15th century writer said of the month:

13

Nowe canst thou reyne, now shyne
And so wrongly drawest the lyne
Nowe art thou hoot, now art thou colde
Nowe canst thou loude and fully blowe,
Nowe smoothe and stilly bere thee lowe,
Nowe canst thou snewe, now canst thou heyle
And us with stormes sore assayle

he reason for 'March many weathers' is that the seas and atmosphere are still cold and 'When the north wind does blow we shall have snow' probably applies more in this month than any other. However, the sun is gaining elevation and given a southerly wind, the land can warm up to a surprising degree.

March 1965 reflected all the vagaries of the month when the mercury plummeted to −7F [−21.7C] on the 3rd in Wales with snow covering much of Britain. But a heatwave at the month's end shot the mercury up to 77F [25C] at Wakefield, Yorkshire.

'Now smoothe and stilly bere thee lowe'

April

Come, gentle Spring!
Ethereal mildness come!

Thompson. The Seasons

Th</sup>here is a welcome freshness to spring and it is said that 'Spring has arrived when a maiden can stand on seven daisies at once'. This is an allusion to soil temperatures which start to rise significantly in April especially on the damp, colder clay soils. The stinging nettle at the back of my garden often displays a surge of growth after mid April.

In 1863, Charles Morran devised the term *'phenology'* – the science of appearances such as the opening of flowers, the coming into leaf of trees and arrival of migrant birds. My own observations in Surrey have shown that spring is extremely variable. In 1989, daffodils were flowering as early as 20th February and there were reports that they were nodding in the breeze at Esher in January 1995. But in both 1986 and 1987 they were not blooming until 2nd April.

April is renowned for its showers. You may have noticed after a clear morning that beautiful 'anvil' clouds have formed high above the fields. Minutes later they are dropping their moisture in a short burst of anger. Occasionally there may be a clap of thunder and the old saying 'Thunder in spring, cold will bring' is often true for these showers frequently form in a chilly polar airstream in northwesterly winds. At night the sky clears with a frosty dawn.

What is this passing scene?
A peevish April day!
A little sun, a little rain,
And then night sweeps along the plain
And all things fade away

Henry White

It is in this type of weather that a rainbow is often seen towards evening. The sun warms the land and thermals rise into the atmosphere, shower clouds form, convection in meteorological terms.

Rainbow to windward, foul falls the day.
Rainbow to leeward, damp runs away.

An evening rainbow is likely to be a better sign than one in the morning. If it occurs early in the day it means the showers are likely to be upwind as our prevailing winds are from a westerly point. Whatever they bring, rainbows are a joyous sight and inspired Wordsworth to write:

My heart leaps up when I behold a rainbow in the sky

However, I have never found a pot of gold at the end of one!

Spring has arrived when a maiden can stand on seven daisies at once !

April, even more so than March, can have both summer and winter embracing it. Classic snowstorms have affected various parts of Britain in the Aprils of 1908, 1919, 1950, 1966 and 1981. Whilst in 1949 the mercury topped over 80F[27C] in southern and eastern England. An old Spanish proverb comes to mind 'April has the face of a monk, but the claws of a cat!'

April can also be more snowy than December:

Christmas in mud,
Easter in snow.

This is not so far fetched. The Boat Race was rowed with spectators watching from snowy banks in 1958. Perhaps this is not a bad thing, for its is said that:

Snow in April is as good as manure.

"Christmas in mud, Easter in snow"

And

April cold and wet fills the barns best yet.

The cool and wet Aprils of 1983 and 1989 were followed by warm and sunny summers.

Altogether, Shakespeare was quite accurate when he wrote:

The uncertain glory of an April day.'

Fine, warm weather early in the season is far from welcomed by farmers and gardeners alike. As explained before, it is no use trees bursting into leaf if sharp frosts then 'scorch' the blossom. The following rhyme was written about apple trees in Somerset's cider orchards:

If your blossom comes in March,
You need not for your barrels search;
If they come in Aparill,
You, may perhaps some barrels fill.
But if your blossom comes in May,
Look out for barrels every day.

"April Showers bring forth May flowers"

18

May

You are as welcome as the flowers in May.

Mackin

Was it always spring weather?
No, we were young and together.

Some weather sayings are born out of good sense and one familiar to all is:

Cast not a clout
'Til May be out.

"Cast not a clout till May is out"

here is some confusion about whether it refers to the may blossom of the hawthorn which flowers around the middle of the month or simply gives the advice: Wait until June arrives. My experience is that the latter is nearer the mark. It is a wise saying since May is very susceptible to cold snaps such as the occasion when a mantle of snow covered the higher parts of Surrey on 2nd May 1979. And looking further back, an icy blast as late as 18th May 1891 led to many trees, shrubs and fruit trees being laid flat by a thick covering of snow across the Midlands and parts of the South East.

He who doffs his coat on a winter's day
Will gladly put it on in May.

This month can bring the first real hot spell of the year but a precaution is needed:

He who bathes in May will soon be laid in clay.

he temptation to plunge into the sea, lakes or rivers is often strong, particularly when the temperature has reached over 90F (32C) but it should be desisted as the water is still cold – around 50F (10C).

The urge to have a dip may be greatest along the South Coast where the beaches enjoy a good deal of sunshine, while inland clouds build up and hide the sun.

The year 1992 saw the following old proverb come true:

A windy March and a rainy April
Make for a beautiful May.

Another version is:

March winds and April showers
Bring forth May flowers.

t my weather station in Surrey, March 1992 brought not one calm day; April was wetter than average whilst May was the warmest since 1833 with plenty of sunshine and flowers.

One piece of weather lore I have never given much credence to is:

> If the oak is out before the ash,
> Then you'll only get a splash.
> But if the ash beats the oak,
> Then you can expect a soak.

Both trees come out in leaf during May and the oak in my locality is often the winner.

The sun now rides high in the sky and if cloud spreads in from the North Sea overnight across eastern England when high pressure lies to the north of Britain, there is no need to worry for it often evaporates, at least away from the chilly coast itself.

> If the evening is red and the morning grey,
> It is a sign of a bonnie day.
> If the evening's grey and the morning red,
> The lamb and the ewe go wet to bed.

More about red skies later.

"He who bathes in May will soon be laid in clay"

21

When mountains and cliffs in sky appear,
some sun but violent showers are near.

June

The month of June is blithe and gay
Driving winter's ills away.

une is often regarded as the lucky month and weatherwise it can boast plenty of sunshine and long days with a gentle warmth that tempted Lowell to write:

And what is so rare as a day in June?
Then, if ever, come perfect days.
Then heaven tries earth if it be in tune
And over it softly her warm ear lays

his is probably the best time to visit the west and north of Scotland, a region renowned for its wind and rain, but a burst of winter did affect many places from the Cairngorms to the Surrey and Kentish downs on 2nd June 1975. An inch of snow forced a cricket match to be abandoned at Buxton, Derbyshire.

It is said that:

A dripping June
Brings all things in tune.

Sometimes Nature can take this far too literally, for in June 1903, in just one week, six inches of rain fell over much of the South East and in the normally dry Chelmsford area of Essex, crops were under six or seven feet of water.

une is one of the most thundery months of the year and a sure sign that a thunderstorm could be on the way is:

When mountains and cliffs in the sky appear,
Some sun but violent showers are near.

23

Less reliable is:

Cats with their tails up and hair apparently
electrified, indicate approaching storm – or a dog!

If the shower is accompanied by thunder, do not stand under the
oak tree.

Beware of the oak, it draws the stroke;
Avoid an ash, it courts the flash.
Creep under the thorn, it will save you from harm.

"Beware of the Oak it draws the stroke,
avoid the Ash it courts the flash,
creep under the thorn it will save you from harm"

24

Studies have shown that oak trees are very susceptible to lightning strikes. For instance, oak trees are hit 60 times more often than beech trees, given an equal number of both. Never stand under one as the main charge of electricity comes *up* from the ground and could pass through you.

In the ferocious thunderstorm of 14th June 1914 at Wandsworth, London, several children died sheltering under a tree.

Towards the end of the month:

> *He who bathes in June*
> *Will sing a merry tune.*

The water is now warming up, but it is not until the end of August or even September that the lakes, seas and rivers are at their warmest.

Thunderstorms apart, let us reflect on the thoughts of another champion of this month, George Macdonald:

> *The roses make the world so sweet;*
> *The bees, the birds have such a tune.*
> *There's such a light, such a heat*
> *And such a joy in June.*

Talking of bees:

> *When bees to distance wing their flight,*
> *Days are warm and skies are bright;*
> *But when their flight ends near the hive,*
> *Wind and rain will surely arrive.*

A Derbyshire saying is quite well-founded:

> *Swarm o' bees i' May*
> *'S worth a load of hay;*
> *Swarm o' bees in June*
> *'S worth a silver spune;*
> *Swarm o' bees in July*
> *'S not worth a fly.*

Bees may have a sensitivity to humidity and electrical activity before thunderstorms or low pressure systems, so a bee line for the hive frequently occurs before inclement summer weather arrives.

The roses make the world so sweet,
The bees, the birds have such a tune,
There's such a light and such a heat
And such a joy in June.

26

July

In this month is St Swithin's Day
On which if that it rain they say
Full forty days after it will
Or more or less some rain distill.

This is one of the most famous of long range weather forecasts and probably the least accurate. Swithin was a ninth century monk who rose to become the Bishop of Winchester. He was a pious, self-effacing man by all accounts, particularly active in restoring churches.

He died in AD 862 and had asked to be buried outside the church 'in a vile and unworthy place, under the drips of eaves, where the sweet rain of heaven may fall on his grave'.

However, his remains were transferred a hundred or so years later to a tomb in a new church in grand ceremony on 15th July though the weather was not mentioned as being tempestuous. But the legend states that a terrific storm raged and rain continued for forty days. Studies carried out in London have shown that the longest spell of consecutive wet days after St Swithin's Day was in 1939 when July 15th was bone dry! The saying does not hold water!

"In a vile and unworthy place under the drips of the eaves
where the sweet rain of heaven may fall"

27

July is another thundery month and lightning can strike the same place twice. Indeed, tall buildings may be struck several times in the same storm. The church steeple of St Mary the Virgin in the Wiltshire village of Steeple Ashton was split by lightning on 25th July 1670. Repair work was nearly complete when, on 15th October that year, it struck again. The steeple collapsed killing two workmen. Eventually the stricken church was restored – but this time without a steeple.

It was Charles II who described an English summer as:

Three fine days and a thunderstorm

There is some truth in this as summer storms are often triggered by an approaching weather front after several fine days which have progressively become hotter. However, the summers of 1976, 1989 and 1990 were surprisingly thunder-free and dominated by high pressure.

Then came hot July, boyling like to fire

July is often the warmest month and probably tempted Winthrop Praed to write in 1833:

I remember, I remember
How my childhood fleeted by;
The mirth of its December,
And the warmth of its July.

Perhaps he was thinking of the hot July of 1808.

Our summer is often maligned. It was Lord Byron who remarked:

The English winter – ending in July
Only to recommence in August

The Reverend Sydney Smith wrote in 1820, "We are all well, and keep large fires as it behoveth those who pass their summers in England."

No doubt the disastrous summer of 1816 was in his mind. This year was dubbed 'the year without a summer' triggered by the massive eruption of the Indonesian volcano Tambora, which pumped its dust into the atmosphere and cooled the climate. This led to poor harvests in Britain.

For all our changeable weather, we do have many a fine July day and the following saying comes to mind as:

> *Swallows high, staying dry,*
> *Swallows low, wet till blow*

There is some truth in this for when the land heats up during the late morning and afternoon, thermals, or upward currents of air carry insects aloft and swallows acrobatically take their high level dinner. Larks, too, with their liquid trilling, enjoy a similar reputation:

> *When they sing long and fly high*
> *Fine weather can be expected to last the day.*

Swallows low, wet till blow.

29

Ants are often prompted into activity by warm, humid weather and the air was thick with flying ants during the early evening of 20th July 1992, preceding a six-hour thunderstorm. It is said of this little creature:

Wise as we are, if we went to their school
There's many a sluggard and many a fool,
Some lessons of wisdom might learn.
They don't wear their time out sleeping or play,
But gather up corn on a sunshine day
And for winter they lay up their stores.
They manage their work in such regular forms
One would think they foresaw all the frost and the storms,
And so brought their food within doors.

They don't wear their time out in sleeping or play,
But gather up corn on a sunshiny day.

August

Rain around Lammas time
When corn begins to fill
Is worth a plough of gold
And all its shares theretill.

he months of July and the first half of August are known as the 'Dog days', so called because the Romans believed that the combined influence of Sirius the Dog Star and the Sun made this the hottest time of the year. Today we know it is the sun gradually warming the atmosphere and the oceans which tends to delay the greatest heat until after Midsummer's Day so it is understandable that August has twice broken the UK temperature record. In 1911 Raunds in Northampton, Epsom in Surrey and Canterbury, Kent all recorded 98F (37C), a figure only beaten on 3rd August 1990 by Cheltenham in Gloucestershire with 99F (37.2C). Dog days indeed!

here is a native annual which flowers during the summer with petals a soft orangy red colour. It has the habit of closing them when the weather clouds over and the humidity reaches 80 per cent. It is called the scarlet pimpernel and is known as the poor man's weather glass. We are told:

Now, look! Our weather glass is spread:
The pimpernel, whose flower
Closes its leaves of spotted red
Against a rainy hour.

ain can arrive especially in showers with the humidity much lower than 80%, but I remember one incident walking through a wood in Surrey during the early afternoon when the petals were tightly closed and just about every forecast was for a dry day to follow, including my own. Dawn the next day revealed ominous cloud, a falling barometer and sure enough, rain duly arrived.

31

We should all look to the sky for our forecast. Little fleecy, puffy, cumulus clouds in the early afternoon mean the weather should generally be set fair.

If woolly fleeces strew the heavenly way,
Be sure, no rain disturbs the summer day.

It is also said that fair weather clouds are 'good humoured'. But when high level, wispy, cirrus clouds progressively invade the sky, beware. If these 'mares' tails' spread in and the wind backs from west to south, give your barometer a tap. If it shows signs of falling, be cautious:

Lowerin' clouds, lowerin' skies;
Stay indoors if you are wise.

'Dry August and warm
Does harvest no harm '.

For those on the Sussex and Hampshire coast, there's a saying:

If you can see the Isle of Wight, it's going to rain.
If it can't be seen, it's raining!

Lundy Isle, too, has the same distinction from Weston Super Mare, but a more general seafaring saying is:

When the wind backs and the glass falls,
Be on your guard 'gainst gales and squalls.

The above is a wise precaution. On 13th and 14th August 1979, the Fastnet Storm was a tragic example of what can happen. With winds gusting over 85 mph, 15 yachts were sunk and 23 abandoned with much loss of life.

Back on land:

A dry August and warm,
Does harvest no harm.

And in spite of any good weather in September:

What August does not boil,
September cannot fry.

'Poor man's weather glass'

33

Low'ring clouds, low'ring skies,
stay indoors if you are wise.

34

September

If weather be fair and tidy thy grain,
Make speedy carriage, for fear of rain.
For tempest and showers deceiveth many
And lingering lubbers lose many a penny.

Thomas Tusser

At this time of year, the evening light lingers long and the sunsets can be very beautiful and give a good clue to the next day's weather:

Red sky at night
Is shepherd's delight.
Red sky in the morning
Is shepherd's warning.

The squirrel gloats on his accomplished hoard.

35

An even, gentle, soft red is what to look for. Not an angry scarlet. Most of our disturbed weather comes in from the west and the upper cloud associated with it can soon blot out the sun. So if you see the sun's orb setting, there is no bad weather for at least 200 miles upstream. The red colour is due to various particles in our atmosphere filtering out the sunlight, allowing only longer wavelengths through and hence the red colour.

A reddish glow in the western sky early morning is not a promising sign for this means approaching bad weather. The sun is reflecting onto the incoming clouds of a low pressure system.

Perhaps the most accurate saying of them all in my experience of sky-gazing is:

A yellow sky to end the day
Means wind and rain is on the way.

Yellow sky shaded a turquoise blue towards the zenith invariably leads to unsettled conditions. Ice crystals, salt particles and water droplets synonymous with approaching bad weather, scatter sunlight and produce the colour. I remember vividly shades of ominous yellow over London and the Home Counties during the late afternoon of Wednesday, 24th January 1990. The next day, Burns Day, a storm struck Britain which resulted in the death of 47 people with winds gusting along the South Coast to over 100 mph.

A further clue to incoming poor weather is a ring or halo around the sun or moon. It is a circle created by refraction of ice crystals associated with those high level cirrus clouds.

If a halo is around the sun or moon,
We can all expect rain soon.

More often, if you look carefully, images of the sun each side of it and at the same elevation, can be seen. Sometimes they are coloured red. Mock suns they are often called – or 'sun dogs' in Norfolk. They can be associated with bad weather cirrus clouds and hence:

Mock sun,
Dry on the run.

36

Certainly these are not signs that farmers and growers want to see at this time of year for:

September blow soft
'til the fruit's in the loft.

Autumn gives us fruit...

October

Autumn gives us fruit;
Summer is comely with crops;
Spring supplies us with flowers;
Winter is alleviated by fire.

Ovid

A spell of two or three fine, warm days in October, such as in 1985 when Cranwell in Lincolnshire recorded 83F (28C) is often referred to as an Indian Summer. The term is thought to have originated in North America where it referred to the fine autumn weather the Indians relied on to harvest any late crops and prepare their communities for the severe winters which are experienced over much of the continent.

T he 18th October is known as St Luke's Little Summer. However, studies carried out in Britain, including my own, do not reveal any special meteorological merits for this date during what is often one of the wettest months of the year. A fine day is welcome at this time of the year when the nights are drawing in and in Sussex, such a fair weather day was known as a 'Weather Breeder'.

This maxim never forget,
To sow dry and set wet,
One for the mouse, one for the crow,
One to rot, and one to grow.

Mony hips and haws,
Mony frosts and snaws.

When dry weather prevails with calm conditions, October can be 'the golden month' with an autumnal display of colour that can justify the Reverend Thomas Constable's lines:

> *Hail, old October, bright and chill,*
> *First freedman from the summer sun!*
> *Spice high the bowl, and drink your fill!*
> *Thank heaven, at last summer's done.*

More often, a seemingly endless conveyor belt of low pressure weather systems cross Britain and some apt sayings spring to mind:

> *First rise after low,*
> *Foretells a stronger blow.*
>
> *Long foretold, long past;*
> *Quick foretold, soon past.*

The strongest winds often occur just as the low pressure area moves away and a rise of pressure takes place in its wake. A quick moving weather system is also soon over and the most famous example of all was the October 1987 Great Storm in Southern England. The mayhem reached a peak in the early hours, followed by the greatest pressure rise ever recorded in the British Isles. By midday, the wind was almost calm and the sun shone.

A good harvest of hips and haws has a reputation of signalling a severe winter. In Scotland, the proverb runs:

> *Mony hips and haws*
> *Mony frosts and snaws.*

If this were true, then the winter of 1989-90 would have rivalled the infamous ones of 1947 or 1963 with deep snow, frozen pipes and even ice floes around the coast. For I observed that autumn a goodly crop of berries; the belief being that Nature provides for birds and wild animals food to withstand a cold spell. Instead we enjoyed a winter on par with the warmest since a record devised in 1659. It is merely a reflection of previous good times earlier in the year and 1989 was very warm and sunny.

October sees many of our migrant birds such as the swallow wing their way to warmer climes. The cuckoo has already departed from our cooling countryside.

In April, cuckoos come;
In May he plays his drum.
In June he changes tune;
In July away he flies.
But heard in September
A thing to remember.
Heard in October,
You're not sober.

'If a halo is around the sun or moon we can all expect rain soon'.

After a big meal, what better way is there to spend an afternoon on a warm, sunny day than to sit down in a soft meadow and ruminate over life's problems. I have found no truth in the old adage that:

Cows and sheep lie down before rain.

Indeed I remember a lovely afternoon at Selborne, Hampshire in May 1990, gazing on a contented couchant herd from the tranquil setting of The Wakes, home of the 18th Century naturalist Gilbert White. Several fine days followed.

On one occasion after I had given a talk on weather lore, a gentleman came up to me and said I had brought back memories of his courting days. He took his girlfriend out for a ride on his motorbike into the country. Not long after reaching rustic haunts, they espied a number of supine cows. His girlfriend cried: "Look, it's going to rain, take me home!" Whereupon he promptly revved up his 500cc Norton and they all stood up. "No, it's not," he said.

Hail, old October, bright and chill. First freedom from the summer sun!

 # November

No warmth, no cheerfulness, no healthful ease;
No comfortable feel in any member.
No shade, no shine, no butterflies, no bees;
No fruits, no flowers, no leaves, no birds.
November.

Thomas Hood

This month was often regarded as being dismal.

Our crowded cities and towns belching forth smoke from countless fires helped to create this image along with the fading daylight. But this is now an overly pessimistic view. With the Clean Air Act inaugurated in London in 1956, for instance, sunshine has dramatically increased and fogs, together with those dreaded smogs, are far less common. In 1991, for example, at the end of November the last roses of summer were picked and the yellow rudbeckia, blue delphinium and mauve pink anemones graced gardens in the south of England. And it is hard to agree with Scott:

November's sky is chill and drear,
November's leaf is red and sear.

There is one saying which is both amusing and not entirely without meteorological content:

If there's ice in November that will bear a duck
There'll be nothing after but sludge and muck.

Put another way, a cold November often means a mild winter to follow. The icy Novembers of 1851, 1871, 1910 and 1919 brought milder conditions in their wake. More recently, it snowed even at Jersey in the Channel Islands as early as Guy Fawkes Day in 1980, and yet the winter was virtually snowless. The weather often comes in cycles with a long period of cold being replaced by one of mild conditions.

St Martin's Day falls on 11th November and tradition has it that the weather is fine and warm. The French proverb says St Martin's summer 'lasts for three days and a bit'. The legend associated with it runs that St Martin, who was the Bishop of Tours, one frosty morning came upon a poor beggar man trembling with the cold. So he gave half his cloak to him and God, in observing this charitable deed, set the sun shining warmly until St Martin could procure another cloak and hence the weather is supposed to be mild at this time of the year. Perhaps Sir John Suckling was thinking about this season when he wrote in the 17th Century:

> *Out upon it, I have loved*
> *Three whole days together;*
> *And am like to love thee more,*
> *If it prove fair weather.*

In Surrey, at least between 1981 and 1991, only 11th November 1985 could be termed cold, so it seems that St Martin is still in favour, or that his size of cloak is difficult to come by!

'If there's ice in November that will bear the weight of a duck,
There'll be nothing after but sludge and muck.'

44

December

O Nature! a' thy shows an' forms
To feeling, pensive hearts hae charms!
Whether the summer kindly warms.
Wi' life and light,
Or winter howls, in gusty storms,
The lang dark night!

Burns – Epistle to William Simpson

It is said that:

A winter fog
Will freeze a dog.

and

Every mile is two in winter.

This was particularly appropriate for London in December 1890 when parts of the capital's centre were completely sun-less with icy, dense fogs on 20 days. As we have seen, these are becoming rare these days, though with light winds and high pressure, a thick, rime-laden fog descended on the capital in December 1991.

The north wind doth blow
And we shall have snow.

This most popular of sayings has become less accurate of late, especially in the south during early winter, yet snow is still very much associated with Christmas. This probably stems back to Charles Dickens' description of the festive season at Dingley Dell in Pickwick Papers, based on the cold, snowy late December of 1829. In Dickens' day, snow was a more frequent visitor to December, but there was absolutely no certainty of it falling on Christmas Day. Judging by recent years, April is as likely as December to see any.

Christmas in mud,
Easter in snow.

This is not as absurd as it may sound.

ore often December is very changeable with a succession of weather systems bringing alternating fine and wet spells, with 'a veering wind bringing fair weather and a backing wind foul'. It is said that 'one fair day in winter makes not birds merry' and that 'a fair day is followed by a mother of a storm'. I suggest that one enjoys a December day with sunshine for St Thomas's Day, the 21st December:

St Thomas grey, St Thomas grey
The longest night and the shortest day.

unshine is at a premium during our winter months as we have already seen. Actually, before the calendar changed in 1752 it was St Lucy's Day, December 13th, and hence:

Lucy light, Lucy light
The shortest day and the longest night.

n weather lore St Thomas's Day has some significance for one is supposed to look at the weathercock at midday when the wind will remain the same for three months. Also, the price of corn was supposed to fall if it froze and rise if it be mild. I have found little significance in this date but 'a green Christmas meant a fat churchyard' has some truth in it, because mild weather out of season is not necessarily a good thing and can interfere with the growing season and the natural rhythm of a plant's flowering and a crop's yield, thus famine and starvation could result. None more so than in 1845-46 when a very cold year was followed by a warm, humid year. The potato famine occurred in Ireland and in Sussex 'great honey dews blighted the plum, cherry and peach and roses were so covered with aphides that they could scarcely come into leaf'.

n recent years with drought never out of the news for long, an old Scottish weather rhyme is very appropriate:

Twixt Martinmas and Yule
Water's wine in every pool.

Rain falling at this time of year is very important for there is little evaporation and ground water supplies are topped up. In summer, with higher temperatures, evaporation dries the soil and rain is not effective in raising underground water levels. Very little rain fell during the 1991-92 winter due to persistent high pressure, and the torrential downpours in Bedfordshire and Herts on 23rd September 1992 did little to 're-start' some dried-up rivers.

One thing we can say is 'spring follows winter', a point Shelley hinted at when he wrote:

> *If winter comes, can*
> *Spring be far behind?*

'Twixt Martinmas and Yule
Water's wine in every pool.'

A 'Dickens Christmas'.

Epilogue

Pride of the dewy morning,
The Swain's experienced eye
From thee takes timely warning
Nor trust the gorgeous sky.

Keble

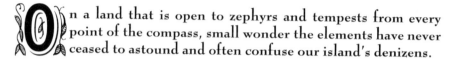n a land that is open to zephyrs and tempests from every point of the compass, small wonder the elements have never ceased to astound and often confuse our island's denizens.

George Ellis in the eighteenth century described the seasons as:

Winter: snowy, flowy, blowy;
Spring: showery, flowery, bowery;
Summer: hoppy, croppy, droppy;
Autumn: breezy, sneezy, freezy.

Shakespeare was less certain when he wrote:

The spring, the summer,
The chiding autumn, angry winter, change
Their wonted liveries and the mazed world
By their increase, now knows not which is which.

Could it have been a massive snowfall as late as the 16th May 1578, when the Bard of Avon was just 14 years old, that shaped those lines from Midsummer Night's Dream?

Whatever the weather, someone always complains or exclaims. Yes, the moon can be blue as it was in December 1883 after the Krakatoa volcanic eruption. But if it rains cats and dogs that's harder to believe. The derivation alludes to the cat being a downpour (perhaps from the French *catadoupe* meaning a waterfall)

49

and the dog a harbinger of wind being an attendant of Odin the storm god from Norse mythology. Yes, someone is always grumbling about the weather, whatever.

The Duke of Rutland urged the folk to pray
For rain; The rain came down the following day.
The pious marvelled, the sceptics murmured fluke,
The farmers late with hay shouted, 'Damn the Duke'.

We have seen how a glance at the sky, or a tap on a barometer can give us an insight as to what may be expected, so avoiding a soggy end to a picnic lunch.

It is said that one day in the 18th century a Doctor Jenner was asked by a lady if he thought it would rain tomorrow. His reply provides a final thought to ponder on:

The hollow winds begin to blow,
The clouds look black, the glass is low;
The soot falls down, the spaniels sleep,
And spiders from their cobwebs peep.
Last night the sun went pale to bed,
The moon in halos hid her head:
The boding shepherd heaves a sigh,
For, see! a rainbow spans the sky:
The walls are damp, the ditches smell,
Closed is the pink-eyed pimpernel.
Hark! how the chairs and tables crack;
Old Betty's joints are on the rack;
Loud quack the ducks, the peacocks cry,
The distant hills are seeming nigh.
How restless are the snorting swine, —
The busy flies disturb the kine.
Low o'er the grass the swallow wings;
The cricket, too, how loud it sings:
Puss on the hearth with velvet paws,
Sits smoothing o'er her whisker'd jaws.
Through the clear stream the fishes rise,
And nimbly catch the incautious flies:

The sheep were seen at early light
Cropping the meads with eager bite.
Though June, the air is cold and chill;
The mellow blackbird's voice is still.
The glow-worms numerous and bright,
Illum'd the dewy dell last night.
At dusk the squalid toad was seen,
Hopping, and crawling o'er the green.
The frog has lost his yellow vest,
And in a dingy suit is dressed.
The leech, disturb'd, is newly risen,
Quite to the summit of his prison.
The whirling winds the dust obeys,
And in the rapid eddy plays;
My dog, so alter'd in his taste,
Quits mutton-bones on grass to feast;
And see you rooks, how odd their flight!
They imitate the gliding kite,
Or seem precipitate to fall,
As if they felt the piercing ball:
'Twill surely rain — I see with sorrow,
Our jaunt must be put off tomorrow.

'Pride of the dewy Morning,
The Swain's experienced eye
From thee takes timely warning
Nor trusts the gorgeous sky.'

51